Cooking with Sauces
Delicious Recipes with Sauces

DEDICATION

Contents

Bechamel Sauce

Ingredients

- 2 tablespoons butter
- 2 tablespoons all-purpose flour
- 1 cup heated milk
- salt to taste
- white pepper to taste
- Optional: freshly ground nutmeg

Steps to Make It

1.   Melt butter in a saucepan or saucier over medium heat. Add flour and stir until mixture is well blended. Cook, stirring constantly, for 2 minutes.
2.   Gradually stir in hot milk. Cook over medium heat, stirring constantly, until sauce begins to boil and thickens.
3.   Simmer, stirring frequently, over very low heat for 5 minutes.
4.   Season with salt and pepper to taste and add a little nutmeg, if desired.

Memphis Barbecue Sauce

Ingredients

- 1 cup/240 mL ketchup

- 1/2 cup/120 mL apple cider vinegar
- 1/2 cup/120 mL water
- 1/4 cup/60 mL onion (pureed)
- 2 tablespoons/30 mL garlic (minced)
- 2 tablespoons/30 mL butter
- 2 tablespoons/30 mL molasses
- 2 tablespoons/30 mL brown sugar
- 1 tablespoons/15 mL prepared mustard
- 1/2 tablespoon/7.5 mL Worcestershire sauce
- 1/2 tablespoon/7.5 mL paprika
- 1/2 tablespoon/7.5 mL mild chili powder
- 2 teaspoons/10 mL dried oregano
- 1 teaspoons/5 mL dried thyme
- 1/2 teaspoon/2.5 mL salt

Steps to Make It

1.   Melt butter in a saucepan over medium heat. Add onion and sauté for 2 to 3 minutes, stirring occasionally. Add garlic and cook for 15 to 20 seconds or until it becomes fragrant. (Do not let the garlic burn or it will cause the sauce to become bitter.)
2.   Add remaining ingredients (vinegar last), reduce heat and simmer over low for 12 to 15 minutes. Stir every so often.
3.   Remove sauce from heat and let cool for 20 minutes.

4.   Use right away or store in an airtight container or jar in the refrigerator for up to one week after preparation.

Remoulade Sauce

Ingredients

- 3/4 cup mayonnaise

- 1 1/2 tablespoons cornichon (finely chopped, or good dill pickle relish)
- 1 teaspoon capers (finely chopped)
- 1 tablespoon lemon juice
- 1 tablespoon mustard (spicy brown or grainy Dijon)
- 2 teaspoon parsley (fresh, chopped)
- Optional: 1/4 teaspoon tarragon (dried leaf)
- 1 dash hot sauce (or to taste)
- 1 pinch salt (or to taste)

Steps to Make It

1. Gather the ingredients.
2. Combine the mayonnaise, chopped cornichon or relish, chopped capers, lemon juice, mustard, parsley, and tarragon, if using.
3. Taste and add hot sauce and salt, as needed.
4. Cover and refrigerate the remoulade sauce until serving time.
5. Serve with your choice of fish, burgers, or as a side for French fries and enjoy!
6.

Chimichurri Sauce

Ingredients

- 1/2 cup water
- 1 teaspoon salt
- 4 to 6 garlic cloves
- 1 cup parsley (or borage or watercress leaves)

- 1/2 cup oregano leaves (or 2 tablespoons dried)
- 2 teaspoons hot pepper flakes (or 1 teaspoon cayenne pepper)
- 1/4 cup red wine vinegar
- 1/2 cup olive oil

Steps to Make It

1. Gather the ingredients.
2. Heat the water and dissolve the salt in it. Remove from heat. When water is cool enough to stick your finger in, proceed with the chimichurri.
3. Put everything except the olive oil into a food processor and pulse to combine. You can puree it or leave it chunky, as you prefer.
4. With the motor running, drizzle in the olive oil and buzz for 30 seconds to a minute. Allow it to marinate for a few hours before serving.
5. Enjoy!

Real Satay Peanut Sauce

Ingredients

- 1 cup fresh dry roasted peanuts (unsalted)
- 1/3 cup water
- 1 to 2 cloves garlic (minced)
- 1/2 teaspoon dark soy sauce
- 2 teaspoon sesame oil
- 2 tablespoons brown sugar

- 1 to 2 tablespoons fish sauce (depending on desired saltiness/flavor; vegetarians substitute 1 1/2 to 2 1/2 tablespoons regular soy sauce)
- 1/2 teaspoon tamarind paste (or 1/2 tablespoon lime juice)
- 1/2 teaspoon cayenne pepper (or 1 teaspoon Thai chili sauce; more or less, to taste)
- 1/3 cup coconut milk

Steps to Make It

1. Gather the ingredients.
2. Place all ingredients in a blender or food processor.
3. Blend or process until sauce is smooth. If you prefer a runnier peanut sauce, add a little more water or coconut milk. Do a taste-test.
4. Serve warm or at room temperature with Thai chicken satay, Thai pork satay or vegetarian/vegan Thai satay.

Easy Caramel Sauce

Ingredients

- 1 1/2 cups brown sugar (packed)
- 4 tablespoons flour
- 1 cup water (boiling)
- Dash salt
- 2 tablespoons butter
- 2 tablespoons heavy cream

- Vanilla (to taste)

Steps to Make It

1. Mix sugar with flour in a saucepan; blend well. Add water and salt.
2. Stir while cooking for 6 to 8 minutes. If too thick add a little more water.
3. Remove from heat; stir in butter, cream, and vanilla to taste.

Bolognese Sauce

Ingredients

- 6 to 8 ounces ground beef (it shouldn't be too lean, or the sugo will be dry)
- Optional: 2 ounces pancetta (minced; if you omit it increase the beef)
- 1 1/2 tablespoons olive oil
- 1/4 medium onion (minced)
- 1/2 carrot (minced)
- 1 stalk celery (minced)
- 1/2 cup red wine (dry)
- 3/4 cup tomatoes (crushed or 2 tablespoons tomato paste dissolved in 1/2 cup water)
- 8 ounces beef broth (If you don't have any, dissolve half a bouillon cube in a cup of boiling water)
- 1 pinch salt
- 1 pound pasta
- Garnish: freshly grated Parmigiano

Steps to Make It

1.   Mince the pancetta and the vegetables, and sauté them in a casserole or Dutch oven with the oil. When the onion is golden, add the ground meat and continue cooking till it's browned.

2.   Stir in the wine and let the sauce simmer till the wine has evaporated, then add the tomatoes, a ladle of broth, and check the seasoning.

3.   Continue simmering over a very low flame for about 2 hours, stirring occasionally, and adding more broth if the sugo looks like it's drying out. The sugo will improve steadily as it cooks, and if you have the time simmer it longer - some suggest it be simmered for 6 hours, adding boiling water or broth as necessary. When it is done it should be rich and thick.

Moroccan Chermoula Marinade

Ingredients

- 1 large bunch cilantro (coriander, finely chopped, only small leaves and small stems)

- 4 cloves garlic (pressed or finely chopped)
- 2 tablespoons paprika
- 1 tablespoon cumin
- 1 teaspoon salt (or more, to taste)
- Optional: 1 teaspoon chopped fresh ginger
- Optional: 1/2 teaspoon cayenne pepper
- 1/4 teaspoon saffron threads (crumbled)
- 3 tablespoons vegetable oil
- 1 small lemon (juiced)

Steps to Make It

1.   Gather the ingredients.
2.   Mix all ingredients in a bowl.
3.   The chermoula is now ready for marinating meats and veggies, dressing potatoes before baking, or mixing into rice, quinoa, or couscous.
4.   Enjoy!

Mexican Chocolate Sauce

Ingredients

- 6 ounces dark chocolate (chopped or grated OR 1/2 cup dark chocolate chips)
- 1/2 cup heavy cream (at room temperature)
- 1 teaspoon cinnamon
- 2 teaspoons coffee liqueur (such as Kahlua)
- 1 tablespoon sugar

Steps to Make It

1.   **Melt the chocolate.** The chocolate does not need to actually cook at all, just melt completely. Use one of the following methods: *Microwave method:* Place chocolate and heavy cream in a microwave safe bowl. Cook in microwave for a minute or so, making sure to stir every 20 seconds. Stop microwaving when mixture is smooth. *Direct stove-top method:* Place chocolate and cream in saucepan over low heat. Stir constantly until mixture is smooth. (Note: Be very careful when using this method, as a moment of inattention can lead to the chocolate's   burning). *Hot water bath method:* Place chocolate and cream in a metal bowl. Place the bowl in pan of very hot water in such a way that the water comes 1/3 to ½ way up the sides of the bowl. Stir ingredients gently until mixture is smooth.

2.   **Stir in** the cinnamon, coffee liqueur, and sugar. Pour into a serving   dish   and   enjoy. Any leftover sauce can be stored in a tightly-covered glass jar in the refrigerator for a week or so. Reheat before using.

Green Goddess Dressing

Ingredients

- 1 1/2 teaspoons anchovy paste
- 1 garlic clove (chopped)

- 3/4 cup fresh parsley leaves (tightly packed)
- 1/2 cup fresh basil or tarragon leaves (tightly packed)
- 1/4 cup fresh chives (tightly packed)
- 2 tablespoons fresh lemon juice
- 1 cup mayonnaise
- 3/4 cup Greek yogurt or sour cream
- Salt and pepper

Steps to Make It

1. Gather the ingredients.
2. Add the anchovy paste, garlic clove, parsley leaves, basil or tarragon leaves, chives, and lemon juice to your blender. Pulse a few times to chop and scrape down the sides.
3. Add the mayonnaise and yogurt or sour cream. Season with salt and pepper. Blend, stopping to scrape down the sides once or twice so that the herbs are fully incorporated, until totally smooth and a bright green color.
4. Serve immediately over salad or as a dipping sauce, or refrigerate in an airtight container for up to 2 days.

Classic Chinese Duck Sauce

Ingredients

- **For the Fruit Mixture:**
- 1 pound plums (halved and pitted)
- 1 pound apricots (halved and pitted)
- 1 cup cider vinegar

- 3/4 cup water
- 1/4 cup balsamic vinegar
- **For the Brown Sugar Mixture:**
- 1 cup cider vinegar
- 1 cup firmly packed brown sugar
- 1 cup white granulated sugar
- 1/2 cup fresh lemon juice
- **For the Spice Mixture:**
- 1/4 cup peeled and chopped ginger
- 1 small onion (sliced thin)
- 1 serrano chile, or more to taste (seeded and chopped)
- 2 garlic cloves (sliced)
- 4 teaspoons kosher salt
- 1 tablespoon toasted mustard seeds
- 1 cinnamon stick

Steps to Make It

1. Make the fruit mixture: Place the plums, apricots, 1 cup cider vinegar, water, and balsamic vinegar in a medium saucepan over medium heat. Bring it to a boil, reduce the heat, and simmer it uncovered for 15 minutes.
2. Make the brown sugar mixture: Place 1 cup of cider vinegar, brown sugar, white sugar, and lemon juice in a separate saucepan.

Bring it to a boil, reduce the heat slightly, and let it bubble for 10 minutes. Let it cool for 5 minutes.

3.   Add the brown sugar mixture to the fruit mixture, along with the ginger, onion, chile, garlic, salt, mustard seeds, and cinnamon stick. Simmer for 45 minutes. Discard the cinnamon stick.

4.   Pour the mixture into a food processor and puree it until smooth. You may need to do this in batches.

5.   Return it to the saucepan and simmer until thickened.

6.   Sterilize a quart-size canning jar or two pint-size canning jars by boiling in a water bath for 15 minutes.

7.   Place the duck sauce in a sterilized canning jar. Cap loosely and let cool to room temperature. Tighten cap and store in a cool, dark place at least 2 weeks before using.

Jamaican Jerk Sauce

Ingredients

- 1/2 cup ground allspice berries
- 1/2 cup packed brown sugar
- 6 to 8 garlic cloves
- 4 to 6 scotch bonnet peppers (seeded and cored)

- 1 tablespoon ground thyme (or 2 tablespoons fresh thyme leaves)
- 2 bunches scallions
- 1 teaspoon cinnamon
- 1/2 teaspoon nutmeg
- Kosher salt (to taste)
- Black pepper (to taste)
- 2 tablespoons soy sauce (to moisten)

Steps to Make It

1. Gather the ingredients.
2. Put all of the ingredients into a food processor or a blender.
3. Process until smooth.
4. Serve and enjoy.

Hollandaise Sauce

Ingredients

- 1 cup clarified butter (about 2 1/2 sticks before clarifying)
- 4 egg yolks
- 1 tablespoon cold water
- 2 tablespoons lemon juice (juice from 1 small lemon), divided
- Kosher salt, to taste

- Cayenne pepper (or a dash of Tabasco sauce, to taste)

Steps to Make It

1. Gather the ingredients.
2. Heat 1 to 2 inches of water in a saucepan over medium heat. Also, make sure your clarified butter is warm but not hot.
3. Combine the egg yolks and the cold water in a glass or stainless steel mixing bowl (not aluminum) and whisk for 1 to 2 minutes, until the mixture is light and foamy. Whisk in a couple of drops of the lemon juice, too.
4. The water in the saucepan should have begun to simmer.
5. Set the bowl directly atop the saucepan of simmering water. The water itself should not come in contact with the bottom of the bowl. Whisk the eggs for 1 to 2 minutes, until they're slightly thickened.
6. Remove the bowl from the heat and begin adding the melted butter slowly at first, a few drops at a time, while whisking constantly. If you add it too quickly, the emulsion will break.
7. Continue beating in the melted butter. As the sauce thickens, you can gradually increase the rate at which you add it, but at first, slower is better.
8. After you've added all the butter, whisk in the remaining lemon juice and season to taste with kosher salt and cayenne pepper (or a dash of Tabasco sauce).

9.   The finished hollandaise sauce will have a smooth, firm consistency. If it's too thick, you can adjust the consistency by whisking in a few drops of warm water.

10.   Serve and enjoy.

Sauce for Crab Cakes

Ingredients

- 1 1/4 cups mayonnaise
- 1/4 cup mustard (Dijon or Creole)
- 1 tablespoon smoked paprika
- 1 teaspoon Creole seasoning
- 1 tablespoon granulated sugar
- 1/2 teaspoon salt
- 1 teaspoon ground black pepper

- 1 clove garlic
- 1 teaspoon capers
- 1 teaspoon lemon juice
- 1 tablespoon parsley
- Optional: 1 tablespoon pickle relish
- Garnish: chopped parsley and chopped dill

Steps to Make It

1. Gather the ingredients.
2. Combine all ingredients except the parsley and dill garnish into a food processor or high-speed blender. Blend until completely smooth.
3. Serve with crispy crab cakes and a salad with a light vinaigrette, and garnish with fresh chopped parsley or dill if you'd like.

Green Schug

Ingredients

- 4 jalapeño peppers
- 4 cloves garlic (peeled)
- 1/2 cup parsley
- 1/2 cup cilantro
- 1 tablespoon lemon juice
- 1/2 teaspoon salt

- 1/4 teaspoon ground cumin
- 1/4 teaspoon ground coriander
- 1/2 cup olive oil

Steps to Make It

1.   Remove the stems from the jalapeño peppers. If you like a very spicy sauce, add them whole to a food processor.
2.   Add the garlic cloves, parsley, cilantro, lemon juice, salt, ground cumin, and ground coriander to the food processor and pulse a few times to chop everything up. With the machine running, pour the olive oil through the feeder tube to create an emulsion. The final sauce should still be a little chunky and have pieces of herbs in it.
3.   Store in an air tight container and serve with pita bread, sour cream or yogurt and grilled vegetables and meat.

Pan Sauce

Ingredients

- 1/2 cup white wine
- Reserved meat juices from cooking
- 1 tablespoons shallots (finely chopped)
- 2 teaspoons Dijon mustard
- 2 teaspoons parsley (chopped fresh)

- 3 tablespoons butter
- Kosher salt (to taste)
- Black pepper (freshly ground, to taste)

Steps to Make It

1. Gather the ingredients.
2. Remove the chicken, pork chops or steak from the pan and let them rest, covered with foil, on a plate in a warm spot. Pour off most of the fat from the pan, but make sure you leave the meat juices. You want a little bit of fat left in the pan to sauté the shallots.
3. Add the chopped shallots to the pan and sauté over medium-high heat until they turn slightly translucent.
4. Now add the wine and scrape all the little toasty bits away from the bottom of the pan with your wooden spoon. Cook for about three minutes or until the wine has reduced by about half.
5. Remove from heat and stir in the mustard and chopped parsley. Finally, whisk in the butter one tablespoon at a time. Season to taste with Kosher salt and spoon the finished pan sauce onto the plate around the meat or chicken.
6. Serve and enjoy!

Turkey (or Chicken) Gravy

Ingredients

- 1 to 2 cups pan drippings (from roasted turkey or chicken or Cornish hens)
- 1/4 cup all-purpose flour
- 1 to 2 cups water (or low sodium or unsalted stock)
- Kosher salt (to taste)
- Black pepper (to taste)

Steps to Make It

1.   Gather the ingredients.
2.   Pour the turkey or chicken pan drippings into a 2-cup measuring cup or gravy separator and skim the fat off.
3.   Put about 1/4 cup of the fat into a saucepan.
4.   Stir in 1/4 cup of all-purpose flour.
5.   Cook, stirring for 2 minutes.
6.   Discard any remaining skimmed fat. Add enough water to the liquids left in the measuring cup to make 2 cups of liquid. Pour the 2 cups of liquid into the flour and fat mixture. Cook, stirring, until thickened and bubbling. Continue cooking for about 1 minute, stirring constantly.
7.   Add kosher salt and freshly ground black pepper to taste.
8.   Enjoy!

Olive Oil Mayonnaise

Ingredients

- 1 egg yolk
- 1 tablespoon freshly squeezed lemon juice
- 1 tablespoon water
- 1 teaspoon Dijon mustard
- 1 cup olive oil (not extra virgin)
- Kosher salt, to taste

Steps to Make It

1.   Place egg yolk, lemon juice, water and mustard in a narrow, tall container. I used a Weck jar. Pour over olive oil, then let the contents settle for a moment.

2.   Using an immersion blender, process until the mayo starts to form. Once you start seeing mayo, gently move the blender up and down. Continue until all oil is emulsified. The texture will be thick.

3.   Season to taste with kosher salt and store in the refrigerator for up to several weeks.

Bearnaise Sauce

Ingredients

- POLENTA CHIPS
- 4 cups vegetable stock
- 1 cup instant polenta
- 1/2 cup grated parmesan
- 2 tbs olive oil
- sea salt

- BEARNAISE SAUCE:
- 1 tbs minced shallot
- 2 tbs fresh tarragon leaves chopped, and their stalks, chopped roughly and bruised
- 2 tbs white wine vinegar
- 2 tbs white wine
- 1 tsp peppercorns crushed or bruised
- 3 egg yolks
- 1 tbs water
- 220 g unsalted butter at room temperature, cut into 1/2-inch cubes, 2 sticks
- Salt
- Freshly milled white or black pepper
- 1/4 to 1/2 lemon juiced
- MUSHROOM STEAKS:
- 4 - 6 extra large portobello mushrooms cleaned and stalks trimmed so that the mushrooms sit flat stalk side down
- 1 tbs olive oil
- salt and pepper

Steps to Make It

1.   Begin by making the polenta chips. Lightly grease a 20cm (8 inch) square cake tin and set aside. Place the stock in a large saucepan over medium heat and bring to the boil. Gradually whisk in the polenta, in a steady stream (don't dump it all in at once), and whisking continuously for 2–3 minutes or until thick. Remove from the heat and stir through the parmesan. Pour into the cake tin carefully smooth the top. Refrigerate for 2 to 3 hours, or overnight, until set.

2.   Preheat the oven to 200 celsius (400 Fahrenheit) and line a baking tray with baking paper or parchment. Remove the polenta from the tin and cut into thick chips. Arrange on the prepared tray and lightly brush with half the olive oil. Bake for 15 minutes and turn the chips and lightly brush with remaining olive oil. Return to the oven and bake until crisp and lightly browned, approximately another 15 minutes. Sprinkle the chips with sea salt and toss to coat.

3.   When the chips go in the oven prepare the bearnaise sauce.

4.   To make the bearnaise, place the shallot, tarragon stalks, half the tarragon leaves, vinegar, white wine and peppercorns in a saucepan. Bring to a boil and reduce until about 1 tbs in volume. Strain the liquid through a tea strainer, and press the tarragon

leaves and stalk to get all of the liquid. Set aside to cool slightly. Place a saucepan of water over a medium heat and bring to a gentle simmer. Place a heatproof bowl over the top of the pan of simmering water (ensuring the bowl does not touch the water) and add the egg yolks and water, along with the tarragon vinegar. Whisk constantly until the mixture thickens and doubles in size start adding the cubes of butter, one at a time, until all the butter is absorbed. Taste and season with salt and pepper along with lemon juice.

5. Just before the chips are ready preheat 2 large frying pans over a medium high heat. Lightly brush the mushrooms with olive oil and sprinkle season with salt and pepper. Cook for 3 to 4 minutes each side, until cooked through and lightly charred.

6. Divide the mushroom steaks and polenta chips between 4 plates. Add the remaining tarragon to the bearnaise and stir through. Serve with the mushroom steaks and chips.

Vinaigrette

Ingredients

- 1 shallot (optional)
- Salt
- 2 tablespoons red wine vinegar
- 5 to 6 tablespoons extra virgin olive oil
- Assorted lettuce greens, amount to taste

Steps to Make It

1.   Peel the shallot and cut into very thin slices. Put in a small bowl with a pinch of salt and the vinegar. Let the shallot soak in the vinegar for 15 to 20 minutes, then stir in the olive oil and mix well. Taste to see if the balance of vinegar and oil is right — you might need to add more of one or the other.

2.   To prepare the lettuces: Remove any damaged leaves on the outside. Separate the heads into individual leaves. Tear large leaves into smaller pieces. Wash them and gently in a bowl in plenty of cold water. Lift the lettuces out and drain.

3.   Spin dry in a salad spinner or lettuce drier. Only fill it half full at a time. The most important thing is to have dry lettuce or the dressing won't coat the leaves. As they are dried spread them out on a

towel. Roll the towel up loosely, put in an airtight bag, and refrigerate until ready to serve.

4.   Toss the salad in the vinaigrette dressing just before serving.

Salsa Verde

Ingredients

- 1/3 cup coarsely chopped parsley (leaves and thin stems only)
- Grated zest of 1 lemon
- 1 small garlic clove, chopped very fine or pounded into a puree
- 1 tablespoon capers, rinsed, drained, and coarsely chopped

- ½ teaspoon salt
- Fresh-ground black pepper to taste
- ½ cup olive oil

Steps to Make It

1.   Combine in a small bowl. Mix well and taste for salt. Let the sauce sit for a while to develop the flavors.

Romesco Sauce

Ingredients

- 1 large roasted red bell pepper from a jar
- 1 garlic clove, smashed
- 1/2 cup slivered almonds, toasted
- 1/4 cup tomato purée
- 2 tablespoons chopped flat-leaf parsley
- 2 tablespoons Sherry vinegar
- 1 teaspoon smoked paprika
- 1/2 teaspoon cayenne pepper

- 1/2 cup extra-virgin olive oil
- Fine sea salt and freshly ground black pepper

Steps to Make It

1. Pulse first 8 ingredients in a food processor until very finely chopped. With motor running, slowly add oil; process until smooth. Season with salt and pepper.

Chimichurri

Ingredients

- 1 c. flat-leaf parsley, firmly packed
- 3 cloves garlic
- 2 tbsp. fresh oregano
- 1/3 c. extra-virgin olive oil
- 1/4 c. red wine vinegar
- 2 tsp. lemon zest (optional)

- Pinch red pepper flakes
- Kosher salt

Steps to Make It

1.   Combine parsley, garlic, and oregano in the bowl of a food processor. Pulse until herbs are finely chopped and garlic is minced.
2.   Transfer herbs to a medium bowl and stir in olive oil, vinegar, and lemon zest if using. Season with salt and a pinch of red pepper flakes.

Espagnole Sauce

Ingredients

- 1 small carrot, coarsely chopped
- 1 medium onion, coarsely chopped
- 1/2 stick (1/4 cup) unsalted butter
- 1/4 cup all-purpose flour
- 4 cups hot beef stock or reconstituted beef-veal demi-glace concentrate*
- 1/4 cup canned tomato purée
- 2 large garlic cloves, coarsely chopped
- 1 celery rib, coarsely chopped

- 1/2 teaspoon whole black peppercorns
- 1 Turkish or 1/2 California bay leaf

Steps to Make It

1.   Cook carrot and onion in butter in a 3-quart heavy saucepan over moderate heat, stirring occasionally, until golden, 7 to 8 minutes. Add flour and cook roux over moderately low heat, stirring constantly, until medium brown, 6 to 10 minutes. Add hot stock in a fast stream, whisking constantly to prevent lumps, then add tomato purée, garlic, celery, peppercorns, and bay leaf and bring to a boil, stirring. Reduce heat and cook at a bare simmer, uncovered, stirring occasionally, until reduced to about 3 cups, about 45 minutes.
2.   Pour sauce through a fine-mesh sieve into a bowl, discarding solids.

Basil Pesto

Ingredients

- ⅓ cup raw pine nuts, almonds, walnuts, pecans or pepitas
- 2 cups packed fresh basil leaves (about 3 ounces or 2 large bunches)
- ¼ cup grated Parmesan cheese
- 1 tablespoon lemon juice
- 2 cloves garlic, roughly chopped

- ½ teaspoon fine sea salt
- ½ cup extra-virgin olive oil

Steps to Make It

1.　(Optional) Toast the nuts or seeds for extra flavor: In a medium skillet, toast the nuts/seeds over medium heat, stirring frequently (don't let them burn!), until nice and fragrant, 3 to 5 minutes. Pour them into a bowl to cool for a few minutes.

2.　To make the pesto, combine the basil, cooled nuts/seeds, Parmesan, lemon juice, garlic and salt in a food processor or blender. With the machine running, slowly drizzle in the olive oil. Continue processing until the mixture is well blended but still has some texture, pausing to scrape down the sides as necessary.

3.　Taste, and adjust if necessary. Add a pinch of salt if the basil tastes too bitter or the pesto needs more zing. Add more Parmesan if you'd like a creamier/cheesier pesto. If desired, you can thin out the pesto with more olive oil. (Consider, however, that if you're serving the pesto on pasta, you can thin it with small splashes of reserved pasta cooking water to bring it all together. See notes for details.)

4.　Store leftover pesto in the refrigerator, covered, for up to 1 week. You can also freeze pesto—my favorite way is in an ice cube try. Once frozen, transfer to a freezer bag, then you can thaw only as much as you need later.

Aioli

Ingredients

- 5 medium cloves garlic, pressed or minced
- 2 teaspoons lemon juice, to taste
- Sprinkle of salt
- ½ cup good quality mayonnaise (I like Sir Kensington's), to taste
- Optional: ¼ teaspoon Dijon mustard

Steps to Make It

1.   In a small, shallow bowl, combine the pressed garlic and lemon juice. Stir to combine and spread it into an even layer so the juice can work its magic. Sprinkle lightly with salt. Let the mixture rest for 10 minutes, so the lemon juice can absorb the garlic's flavor.

2.   Place a fine mesh strainer over another bowl. Using a silicone or rubber spatula, scoop the contents of the bowl into the strainer, then press on the garlic with the spatula to get as much juice out as possible. Discard the garlic.

3.   Stir the mayo into the garlicky lemon juice until combined. Taste, and adjust only if necessary—if the garlic flavor is overwhelming, stir in more mayonnaise by the tablespoon. If you want it to taste a little more interesting, add the Dijon mustard. For more tang, add another little squeeze of lemon juice.

4.   Aioli will keep well in the refrigerator, covered, for up to 10 days. It will thicken up more as it chills.

Red Wine Sauce

Ingredients

- 1 cup red wine
- 2 tablespoons cold butter, cut up
- Coarse salt

Steps to Make It

1.   Place 1 cup red wine in a small saucepan; boil until reduced to 1/4 cup, 8 to 10 minutes.

2.   Remove from heat; add 2 tablespoons cold cut-up butter, and swirl pan until butter is melted and sauce is thickened, about 1 minute. Season with coarse salt; serve with Pepper-Crusted Filet Mignon.

Balsamic Fig Sauce

Ingredients

- 1 pound fresh figs, preferably Black Mission, chopped into 3/4-inch pieces.

- 1/3 cup red wine.
- 1 tablespoon balsamic vinegar, or to taste.
- Pinch of salt.
- 1/8 teaspoon freshly ground black pepper.
- 1/2 teaspoon sugar.
- 1 sprig fresh thyme.

Steps to Make It

1. Combine all ingredients with 1/2 cup water in a small saucepan. Cover; bring to a boil over high heat. Reduce to a simmer; cook, partially covered, until fruit has broken down, 20 to 30 minutes.

2. Let cool slightly; remove thyme sprig. Press mixture through a large-holed sieve with a rubber spatula.

Stir-Fry Sauce

Ingredients

- 2 cloves garlic, minced
- 1 tablespoon fresh ginger, chopped fine
- 1 teaspoon sesame oil
- 2 tablespoons rice vinegar
- 1/4 cup soy sauce

- 1/4 cup chicken broth, vegetable broth or even water
- 1 tablespoon sriracha
- 2 tablespoons sugar
- 1 tablespoon cornstarch

Steps to Make It

1. Combine all ingredients in a small bowl or Tupperware and mix well

2. Stir fry about 2 cups any combination of diced vegetables and/or seafood, chicken or beef until protein is just cooked through

3. When just done, add 1/2 to 2/3 of sauce, mix and let thicken slightly – about a minute and serve

Adobo-Honey Sauce

Ingredients

- 2/3 cup of plain honey
- 1 teaspoon adobo sauce

Steps to Make It

1.   Warm the honey if necessary so it flows easily. A few second in the microwave will work. You need it flowing, not hot.

2.   Add the adobo sauce and carefully mix to ensure uniformity. Taste test and, if you desire, add more fire. Just remember, you can make it hotter but you can only make it cooler by diluting with additional honey.

Marinara Sauce

Ingredients

- 1 large can (28 ounces) whole peeled tomatoes*
- 1 medium yellow onion, peeled and halved
- 2 large cloves garlic, peeled but left whole
- 2 tablespoons extra-virgin olive oil
- 1 teaspoon dried oregano
- Pinch of red pepper flakes (optional, omit if sensitive to spice)
- Salt, to taste (if necessary)

- Optional, for serving: Cooked pasta, grated Parmesan cheese or vegan Parmesan, chopped fresh basil, additional olive oil

Steps to Make It

1. In a medium, heavy-bottomed saucepan, combine the tomatoes (with their juices), halved onion, garlic cloves, olive oil, oregano and red pepper flakes (if using).
2. Bring the sauce to a simmer over medium-high heat, then lower the heat to keep the sauce at a slow, steady simmer for about 45 minutes, or until droplets of oil float free of the tomatoes. Stir occasionally, and use a sturdy wooden spoon to crush the tomatoes against the side of the pot after about 15 minutes has passed.
3. Remove the pot from the heat and discard the onion. Smash the garlic cloves against the side of the pot with a fork, then stir the smashed garlic into the sauce. Do the same with any tiny onion pieces you might find. Use the wooden spoon to crush the tomatoes to your liking (you can blend this sauce smooth with an immersion blender or stand blender, if desired).
4. Add salt, to taste (the tomatoes are already pretty salty, so you might just need a pinch). Serve warm. This sauce keeps well, covered and refrigerated, for up to 4 days. Freeze it for up to 6 months.

Cooking with Sauces

Printed in Great Britain
by Amazon